Little

Book

Of

Investment

Quotes

Thank you to all of the amazing investors, traders, CEOs, thinkers, dreamers, doers, and world changers that have inspired me throughout my investing career.

I am constantly striving to learn more and improve myself in every aspect of life. Investing is an incredible passion of mine that started out as a hobby and morphed into my career.

Entire fortunes have been made and lost in the stock market. I have found that borrowing wisdom from investing experts is a great way to start every day. I wish you nothing but the best on your journey through life.

This book contains a list of 365+ investing quotes from all over the world to help motivate, inspire, and push you to become the best investor you can possibly be.

These quotes come from a wide range of successful investors, traders, financial advisors and industry leaders.

Read one every morning to start your day off on the right foot in a positive mindset before the market has a chance to beat you down and play with your emotions.

The most powerful way to improve your investment performance is to first change your way of thinking, and this book will help you with that. Read a quote every day, absorbing knowledge from the world's best investors!

"An investment in knowledge pays the best interest."
—Benjamin Franklin

1. The realization that you are responsible for your results is the key to successful investing. Winners know they are responsible for their results; losers think they are not. -Dr. Van K. Tharp

2. Those who are unwilling to invest in the future haven't earned one. -H.W. Lewis

3. I've always loved to play games, and face it: investing is one big game. You need to be decisive, open-minded, flexible and competitive. -Stanley Druckenmiller

4. Invest for the long term. -Lou Simpson

5. Wide diversification is only required when investors do not understand what they are doing. -Warren Buffett

6. You get out of an investment what you put into it, so the first decision you have to make is how much time you are prepared to devote to the initial task of acquiring a basic knowledge of investments.
-James D. Slater

7. I've been in a hurry all my life. I've been in a hurry to succeed, and in a hurry to prove myself. -Henry Kravis

8. The key to making money in stocks is not to get scared out of them. –Peter Lynch

9. To make money in the stock market, you either have to be ahead of the crowd or very sure they are going in the same direction for some time to come. –Gerald Loeb

10. An investor without investment objectives is like a traveler without a destination. –Ralph Seger

11. Never trade impulsively, especially on other people's advice. –Stuart Walton

12. Good traders consistently take profits on their positions and they stop out of trades quickly when they're going the wrong way. -Jeff Clark

13. Everyone always wants to hold on to their stocks. They irrationally want to hold on to stocks that have made them money, and they irrationally want to hold on to stocks that have lost them money. If you want to invest well, you have to acknowledge that irrationality and combat it with discipline. -Jim Cramer

14. Markets often rise higher than you think is possible, and fall lower than you can possibly imagine.

    –Jim Rogers

15. Don't try to be a jack of all investments. Stick to the field you know best.

    –Bernard Baruch

16. Where there is smoke, there is fire, or there is never just one cockroach. In other words, bad news is usually not a one-time event; more usually follows.

    –Arthur Huprich

17. Even the intelligent investor is likely to need considerable willpower to keep from following the crowd.
-Benjamin Graham

18. Risk control is the most important thing in trading.
-Paul Tudor Jones

19. One of the biggest mistakes novice investors make is ignoring proper position sizing. When I say position sizing, I mean how much of your portfolio you put into each investment.
-Dr. David Eifrig, Jr.

20. Markets tend to return to the mean over time. -Robert Farrell

21. It's not how much money you make, but how much money you keep, how hard it works for you, and how many generations you keep it for. -Robert Kiyosak

22. It never was my thinking that made big money for me. It was always my sitting. Got that? My sitting tight! -Jesse Livermore

23. Fear and greed are stronger than long-term resolve. -Robert Farrell

24. One of the big problems with growth investing is that we can't estimate earnings very well. I really want to buy growth at value prices. I always look at trailing earnings when I judge stocks. -David Dreman

25. Always insist on a margin of safety. -James Montier

26. More than anything else, what differentiates people who live up to their potential from those who don't is a willingness to look at themselves and others objectively. -Ray Dalio

27. Do not buy the hype from Wall Street and the press that stocks always go up. There are long periods when stocks do nothing and other investments are better.
-Jim Rogers

28. The secret to investing is to figure out the value of something... and then pay a lot less. -Joel Greenblatt

29. If a historically accepted investment yardstick proves to be overly restrictive, the path of least resistance is to invent a new standard.
-Seth Klarman

30. Since the market tends to go in the opposite direction of what the majority of people think, I would say 95% of all these people you hear on TV shows are giving you their personal opinion. And personal opinions are almost always worthless... facts and markets are far more reliable.
    -William J. O'Neil

31. The surest way to make money is to buy your own dollar bills for $0.80 or $0.90. -Warren Buffett

32. A losing trader can do little to transform himself into a winning trader. A losing trader is not going to want to transform himself. That's the kind of thing winning traders do. –Ed Seykota

33. Don't try to buy at the bottom and sell at the top. This can't be done... except by liars. –Bernard Baruch

34. CEOs are paid for doing a terrible job. If the system wasn't so messed up, guys like me wouldn't make this kind of money. –Carl Icahn

35. The future is uncertain; it is always a difficult time to invest. –John Griffin

36. The average man doesn't wish to be told that it is a bull or a bear market. What he desires is to be told specifically which particular stock to buy or sell. He wants to get something for nothing. He does not wish to work. He doesn't even wish to have to think.
–Jesse Livermore

37. Don't invest your money on the advice of a poor man.
–Spain

38. Remember, it's the quality of your ideas, not the quantity that will result in the big money.
   -Joel Greenblatt

39. Be who you are and say what you feel, because those who mind don't matter, and those who matter don't mind. -Bernard Baruch

40. Bull markets are born on pessimism, grown on skepticism, mature on optimism and die on euphoria.
   -Sir John Templeton

41. Face up to two unpleasant facts: the future is never clear; you pay a very high price in the stock market for a cheery consensus. Uncertainty actually is the friend of the buyer of long-term values.
–Warren Buffett

42. The lesson of Buffett is: to succeed in a spectacular fashion you have to be spectacularly unusual.
–Michael Burry

43. Never average losses.
–Jesse Livermore

44. I don't want a lot of good investments; I want a few outstanding ones.
-Philip Fisher

45. When all the experts and forecasts agree... something else is going to happen.
-Robert Farrell

46. The real money made in speculating has been in commitments showing a profit right from the start.
-Jesse Livermore

47. Pay only a reasonable price, even for an excellent business. -Lou Simpson

48. Once we realize that imperfect understanding is the human condition, there is no shame in being wrong, only in failing to correct our mistakes. -George Soros

49. I think a lot of funds get their ideas from Wall Street. I just like to find my own ideas. I read a lot. A lot of news. I just follow my nose. A lot of times it's a dead end, but sometimes there's value there. -Michael Burry

50. Remain confident... the opportunities never stop. -Stuart Walton

51. Go for a business that any idiot can run — because sooner or later, any idiot is probably going to run it.
-Peter Lynch

52. I often remind our analysts that 100% of the information you have about a company represents the past, and 100% of a stock's valuation depends on the future. -Bill Miller

53. It's far better to buy a wonderful company at a fair price than a fair company at a wonderful price.
-Warren Buffett

54. No investment should ever be considered sacred when a better one comes along.
-Seth Klarman

55. If you have trouble imagining a 20% loss in the stock market, you shouldn't be in stocks. -John Bogle

56. Security prices sometimes fluctuate, not based on any apparent changes in reality, but on changes in investor perception. In the short run, supply and demand alone determine the market prices. -Seth Klarman

57. Valuation tells how compressed the spring is, but not when the trigger is released. -Stuart Walton

58. Value investing by its very nature is contrarian. Out-of-favor securities may be undervalued; popular securities almost never are. What the herd is buying is, by definition, in favor. Securities in favor have already been bid up in price on the basis of optimistic expectations and are unlikely to represent good value that has been overlooked. -Seth Klarman

59. Successful investors tend to be unemotional, allowing the greed and fear of others to play into their hands. By having confidence in their own analysis and judgment, they respond to market forces not with blind emotion, but with calculated reason. –Seth Klarman

60. The public is often right during the trends, but wrong at both ends. –Humphrey Neill

61. Listen to the market, not outside opinions. –Stuart Walton

62. Capitalism without financial failure is not capitalism at all, but a kind of socialism for the rich. -James Grant

63. In addition to many other contributing factors of inflation or deflation, a very great factor is the psychological. The fact that people think prices are going to advance or decline very much contributes to their movement, and the very momentum of the trend itself tends to perpetuate itself. -Gerald Loeb

64. Don't let the opinions of the average man sway you. Dream, and he thinks you're crazy. Succeed, and he thinks you're lucky. Acquire wealth, and he thinks you're greedy. Pay no attention. He simply doesn't understand.
−Robert G. Allen

65. Look down, not up, when making your initial investment decision. If you don't lose money, most of the remaining alternatives are good ones.
−Joel Greenblatt

66. Look past tomorrow; develop a six-month and one-year outlook.
-Stuart Walton

67. If you cannot make money out of the leading active issues, you are not going to make money out of the stock market as a whole.
-Jesse Livermore

68. I don't judge success, I celebrate it. I think success has to do with finding and following one's calling, regardless of financial gain.
-Ed Seykota

69. Successful stocks don't tell you when to sell. When you feel like bragging, it's probably time to sell.
–John Neff

70. Bad luck can befall you; mistakes happen. The river may overflow its banks only once or twice in a century, but you still buy flood insurance on your house each year. –Seth Klarman

71. Behold the turtle. He makes progress only when he sticks his neck out.
–James Bryant Conant

72. In essence, the stock market represents three separate categories of business. They are, adjusted for inflation: those with shrinking intrinsic value, those with approximately stable intrinsic value, and those with steadily growing intrinsic value. The preference, always, would be to buy a long-term franchise at a substantial discount from growing intrinsic value.
-Michael Burry

73. You should always be eager to take profits! -Jim Cramer

74. When you stop thinking — not believing, thinking — that a stock you own will go higher, you sell it. Not all at once, but incrementally.
-Jim Cramer

75. Make a periodic reappraisal of all your investments to see whether changing developments have altered their prospects.
-Bernard Baruch

76. Nothing new ever occurs in the business of speculating or investing in securities and commodities.
-Jesse Livermore

77. We will never become dependent on the kindness of strangers. We will always arrange our affairs so that any requirements for cash we many conceivably have will be dwarfed by our own liquidity. Moreover, that liquidity will be constantly refreshed by a gusher of earnings from our many and diverse businesses.
    -Warren Buffett

78. Every once in a while, the market does something so stupid it takes your breath away. -Jim Cramer

79. When it comes to selling stocks, it is plain that nobody can sell unless somebody wants those stocks. If you operate on a large scale, you will have to bear that in mind all the time. –Jesse Livermore

80. A corollary to the importance of compounding is that it is very difficult to recover from even one large loss, which could literally destroy all at once the beneficial effects of many years of investment success. –Seth Klarman

81. Before you buy a security, find out everything you can about the company, its management and competitors, its earnings and possibilities for growth.
-Bernard Baruch

82. Since security prices reflect investors' perception of reality and not necessarily reality itself, overvaluation may persist for a long time.
-Seth Klarman

83. I wait until an investment idea is so good, it hits me over the head like an anvil.
-Joel Greenblatt

84. My experience with novice traders is that they trade three to five times too big. They are taking 5 to 10 percent risks on a trade when they should be taking 1 to 2 percent risks. The emotional burden of trading is substantial; on any given day, I could lose millions of dollars. If you personalize these losses, you can't trade.
-Bruce Kovner

85. Investors who buy and sell based on media or analyst commentary are not for us.
-Warren Buffett

86. A lot of people have the wrong attitude... they want to see how far they can ride the stock up. That's undisciplined and it will lose you money. -Jim Cramer

87. I remember my sense of shock some half-dozen years ago when I read a [stock] recommendation to sell shares of a company... The recommendation was not based on any long-term fundamentals. Rather, it was that over the next six months the funds could be employed more profitably elsewhere. -Philip Fisher

88. Even with a margin [of safety] in the investor's favor, an individual security may work out badly. For the margin guarantees only that he has a better chance for profit than for loss... not that loss is impossible. But as the number of such commitments is increased, the more certain does it become that the aggregate of the profits will exceed the aggregate of the losses.
    –Benjamin Graham

89. Sell when you *can*, not when you *have to*.
    –Arthur Huprich

90. This company looks cheap, that company looks cheap, but the overall economy could completely screw it up. The key is to wait. Sometimes the hardest thing to do is to do nothing.
   -David Tepper

91. The fact that people will be full of greed, fear, or folly is predictable. The sequence is not predictable.
   -Warren Buffett

92. If you spend more than 13 minutes analyzing economic and market forecasts, you've wasted 10 minutes.
   -Peter Lynch

93. Value investors look at cash flows. If a company can maintain present cash flows for 5 or 6 years, it's a good investment. Investors then just hope that those cash flows—and thus the company's value—don't decrease faster than they anticipate. -Peter Thiel

94. I trust my own instinct and experience that I gained over years and the feeling when the moment is right for buying shares. That is what one calls intuition. -Alisher Usmanov

95. In the end, what counts in investing is what you pay for a business — through the purchase of a small piece of it in the stock market, and what that business earns in the succeeding decade or two. -Warren Buffett

96. Accepting losses is the most important single investment device to insure safety of capital. -Gerald Loeb

97. Be prepared for disappointment and frustration. Be persistent and bounce back even more determined to succeed. -Paul Clitheroe

98. There is nothing new on Wall Street. There can't be because speculation is as old as the hills. Whatever happens in the stock market today has happened before and will happen again, mostly due to human nature. -Arthur Huprich

99. I know that to be successful [in trading], I have to be frightened.
-Paul Tudor Jones

100. The individual investor should act consistently as an investor and not as a speculator.
-Benjamin Graham

101. Do not diversify excessively.
-Lou Simpson

102. You might own a stock that has doubled since you bought it, but you can't honestly say you've made money in a stock until you sell the stock and cash out.
-Jim Cramer

103. It's waiting that helps you as an investor, and a lot of people just can't stand to wait. If you didn't get the deferred-gratification gene, you've got to work very hard to overcome that. -Charlie Munger

104. Understand the big picture. –George Soros

105. Somehow, in a business [securities trading] so ephemeral, the notion of going home each day, for as many days as possible, having made a profit — that's what was so satisfying to me. –Michael Steinhardt

106. Adding to losers is easy but usually wrong. –Stuart Walton

107. Never sell a stock because it seems high-priced. –Jesse Livermore

108. Emphasis on the junior claims against a company is a greater-fool argument, wherein one takes comfort from the potentially foolish actions of others rather than from the wisdom of one's own. –Seth Klarman

109. Force yourself to trade against the consensus. –Stuart Walton

110. Your odds of success improve when you buy stocks when the technical pattern confirms the fundamental opinion. –Arthur Huprich

111. Force yourself to buy on extreme weakness and sell on extreme strength.
    –Stuart Walton

112. Psychology is probably the most important factor in the market... and one that is least understood.
    –David Dreman

113. Learn how to take your losses quickly and cleanly. Don't expect to be right all the time. If you have made a mistake, cut your losses as quickly as possible.
    –Bernard Baruch

114. As a speculator, you must embrace disorder and chaos. –Louis Bacon

115. One useful fact to remember is that the most important indications are made in the early stages of a broad market move. Nine times out of ten, the leaders of an advance are the stocks that make new highs ahead of the averages. –Gerald Loeb

116. Start each day from last night's close, not your original cost.
–Stuart Walton

117. Profits always take care of themselves but losses never do. –Jesse Livermore

118. Make great returns by avoiding mistakes.
     –Peter Peterson

119. No one can see ahead three years, let alone five or ten. Competition, new inventions - all kinds of things - can change the situation in twelve months.
     –Thomas Rowe Price, Jr.

120. It is much easier to watch a few than many.
     –Jesse Livermore

121. A correction takes place to determine which investments are the tennis balls and which are the eggs. You want to own the things that bounce (as in tennis balls) and not eggs. -William Berger

122. Dramatic and emotional trading experiences tend to be negative. Pride is a great banana peel, as are hope, fear, and greed. My biggest slip-ups occurred shortly after I got emotionally involved with positions. -Ed Seykota

123. Stay focused, especially when the markets are moving. –Stuart Walton

124. We do a lot of thinking and not a lot of acting. A lot of investors do a lot of acting and not a lot of thinking. –Lou Simpson

125. This time is *never* different. –James Montier

126. To achieve satisfactory investment results is easier than most people realize; to achieve superior results is harder than it looks. –Benjamin Graham

127. It is absurd to think that the general public can ever make money out of market forecasts.

–Benjamin Graham

128. Bull markets are more fun than bear markets.

–Robert Farrell

129. When buying shares, ask yourself, would you buy the whole company?

–Rene Rivkin

130. Don't focus on making money. Focus on protecting what you have.

–Paul Tudor Jones

131. Realize that a loss in the stock market is part of the investment process. The key is not letting it turn into a big one as this could devastate a portfolio.
    –Arthur Huprich

132. Avoid businesses whose futures you can't evaluate, no matter how exciting their products may be.
    –Warren Buffett

133. Don't make investment or trading decisions based on tips. Tips are something you leave for good service.
    –Arthur Huprich

134. It's not always easy to do what's not popular, but that's where you make your money. Buy stocks that look bad to less careful investors and hang on until their real value is recognized. –John Neff

135. Think independently. –Lou Simpson

136. I do an enormous amount of trading, not necessarily just for profit, but also because it opens up other opportunities. I get a chance to smell a lot of things. Trading is a catalyst. –Michael Steinhardt

137. How many millionaires do you know who have become wealthy by investing in savings accounts? I rest my case.
    -Robert G. Allen

138. Don't average trading losses, meaning don't put "good" money after "bad." Adding to a losing position will lead to ruin. Ask the Nobel Laureates of Long Term Capital Management.
    -Arthur Huprich

139. Invest in yourself. Your career is the engine of your wealth.
    -Paul Clitheroe

140. Having a quote machine is like having a slot machine at your desk... you end up feeding it all day long. I get my price data after the close each day.
-Ed Seykota

141. The market does not trade upon what everybody knows, but upon what those with the best information can foresee.
-William Hamilton

142. When most investors, including the pros, all agree on something, they're usually wrong.
-Carl Icahn

143. The research task does not end with the discovery of an apparent bargain. It is incumbent on investors to try to find out why the bargain has become available. –Seth Klarman

144. Willingness and ability to hold funds in cash while awaiting real opportunities is a key to success in the battle for investment survival. –Gerald Loeb

145. Portfolios heavy with underperforming stocks rarely outperform the stock market!
    –Arthur Huprich

146. Never let a profitable trade turn into a loss, and never let an initial trading position turn into a long-term one because it is at a loss. -Arthur Huprich

147. Profits can be made safely only when the opportunity is available and not just because they happen to be desired or needed.
-Gerald Loeb

148. If you're running a business for the long term, the last thing you should be doing is borrowing money to buy back stock.
-Stanley Druckenmiller

149. When trading, if a stock doesn't perform as expected within a short time period, either close it out or tighten your stop-loss point. –Arthur Huprich

150. You get recessions... you have stock market declines. If you don't understand that's going to happen, then you're not ready... you won't do well in the markets. –Peter Lynch

151. In general, markets know more than the people who write about them. –James Grant

152. When you have tremendous conviction on a trade, you have to go for the jugular. It takes courage to be a pig. -Stanley Druckenmiller

153. In any sort of contest — financial, mental, or physical — it's an enormous advantage to have opponents who have been taught it's useless to even try. -Warren Buffett

154. It is not good to be too curious about all the reasons behind price movements.

-Jesse Livermore

155. We can't control the stock market. The very best we can do is to try to understand what the stock market is trying to tell us.
–Arthur Huprich

156. Those of us who have been very fortunate have a duty to give back. Whether one gives a lot as one goes along as I do, or a little and then a lot (when one dies) as Warren does, is a matter of personal preference.
–Charlie Munger

157. Get rid of all distractions.
–Stuart Walton

158. One lucky break, or one supremely shrewd decision may account for more than a lifetime of journeyman efforts. But behind the luck or crucial decision there must usually exist a background of preparation and disciplined capacity.
-Benjamin Graham

159. As long as a stock is acting right and the market is "in-gear", don't be in a hurry to take a profit on the whole position. Scale out instead.
-Arthur Huprich

160. Make sure you've got a great elevator pitch for your investment idea.
–Julian Robertson

161. The idea of *anticipation* is key to investing and to business generally. You can't wait for an opportunity to become obvious. You have to think, "Here's what other people and companies have done under certain circumstances. Now, under these new circumstances, how is this management likely to behave?"
–Eddie Lampert

162. Be contrarian.
-James Montier

163. Never play macho man
with the market.
-Paul Tudor Jones

164. Pursuing your passion is
fulfilling and leads to
financial freedom.
-Robert G. Allen

165. If you stay half-alert, you
can pick the spectacular
performers right from
your place of business or
out of the neighborhood
shopping mall, and long
before Wall Street discovers
them. -Peter Lynch

166. I always used fundamentals. But the fact is that often, the time frame of my investments was short-term. –Michael Steinhardt

167. The liabilities are always 100 percent good. It's the assets you have to worry about. –Charlie Munger

168. Trade on your own ideas and style. –Stuart Walton

169. Beware of barbers, beauticians, and waiters... of anyone bringing gifts of "inside" information or "tips." –Bernard Baruch

170. Think trades through, including profit/loss exit points, before you put them on. -Stuart Walton

171. Do you really like a particular stock? Put 10% or so of your portfolio on it. Make the idea count... Good [investment] ideas should not be diversified away into meaningless oblivion. -Bill Gross

172. In order of importance to me are: 1) the long term trend, 2) the current chart pattern and 3) picking a good spot to buy or sell. -Ed Seykota

173. The first principle is that you must not fool yourself... and you are the easiest person to fool.
-Richard Feynman

174. Markets are never wrong... opinions often are.
-Jesse Livermore

175. Huge sums have been lost by investors who have held on to securities after the reason for owning them is no longer valid. In investing it is never wrong to change your mind. It is only wrong to change your mind and do nothing about it. -Seth Klarman

176. It is ludicrous to believe that asset bubbles can only be recognized in hindsight. -Michael Burry

177. The amount of money you have has got nothing to do with what you earn... people earning a million dollars a year can have no money and people earning $35,000 a year can be quite well off. It's not what you earn, it's what you spend. -Paul Clitheroe

178. Fallible emotional people determine price; cold hard cash determines value. -Christopher C. Davis

179. Investors are sometimes their own worst enemies. When prices are generally rising, for example, greed leads investors to speculate, to make substantial, high-risk bets based upon optimistic predictions, and to focus on return while ignoring risk. At the other end of the emotional spectrum, when prices are generally falling, fear of loss causes investors to focus solely on the possibility of continued price declines to the exclusion of investment fundamentals.

-Seth Klarman

180. If you learn to take the emotions out of the equation, you can become a very successful trader (or investor) no matter how you define it. –Jeff Clark

181. Never bet on the end of the world. It only happens once. –Art Cashin

182. We all like to think that we're smart, and that we can make rational, logical decisions unaffected by emotion. Those are the characteristics of good investors... but they apply to very few of us.
–Jeff Clark

183. Your ultimate success or failure will depend on your ability to ignore the worries of the world long enough to allow your investments to succeed.
-Peter Lynch

184. The herd instinct is the strongest emotion; especially dangerous in investing. -Unknown

185. Persist... don't take no for an answer. If you're happy to sit at your desk and not take any risk, you'll be sitting at your desk for the next 20 years.
-David Rubenstein

186. Bottoms in the investment world don't end with four-year lows; they end with 10- or 15-year lows. –Jim Rogers

187. Do not become completely bearish or bullish on the whole market because one stock in some particular group has plainly reversed its course from the general trend. –Jesse Livermore

188. You have to be patient and wait for the right setup before getting aggressive on any particular trade. Proper timing is critical for a trader. –Jeff Clark

189. What seems too high and risky to the majority generally goes higher and what seems low and cheap generally goes lower.
—William J. O'Neil

190. The first bad bank loan was no doubt made around the time of the opening of the first bank.
—James Grant

191. Demand excellence of yourself. Don't cut corners.
—Stephen Schwarzman

192. Volatility creates the opportunity.
—James Montier

193. Avoiding losses is the most important prerequisite to investment success.
-Seth Klarman

194. Great investors are not unemotional, but are inversely emotional — they get worried when the market is up and feel good when everyone is worried.
-Bill Miller

195. I never allow myself to have an opinion on anything that I don't know the other side's argument better than they do.
-Charlie Munger

196. Try to ignore near-term market fluctuations. If you intend to be invested for a five-year or longer period, the true risk is in not owning stocks or similar investments that appreciate faster than the rate of inflation over time. -David Dreman

197. There are two times when people forget their principles: at the top of the market and at the bottom. -Phillip A. Lowe

198. Leverage limits staying power. -James Montier

199. Companies that meet our criteria are difficult to find. When we think he have found one, we make a large commitment.
   –Lou Simpson

200. I can't emphasize enough the importance of staying with the trend in the market, being in gear with the tape, and not fighting the major movements. Fighting the tape is an invitation to disaster.
   –Martin Zweig

201. Shorts are not more or less evil than longs.
   –Stuart Walton

202. As long as a stock is acting right, and the market is right, do not be in a hurry to take profits.
–Jesse Livermore

203. I have to limit the size of my trading account to an amount that I can be unemotional about.
–Jeff Clark

204. We don't have to be smarter than the rest. We have to be more disciplined than the rest.
–Warren Buffett

205. Buy right and hold tight.
–John Bogle

206. There are two main drivers of asset class returns: inflation and growth. -Ray Dalio

207. Excesses in one direction will lead to an opposite excess in the other direction. -Robert Farrell

208. Don't trust your own opinion and back your judgment until the action of the market itself confirms your opinion. -Jesse Livermore

209. Be patient... wait for the opportunity. -Stuart Walton

210. Respect the difficulty of working with a mass of information. Few of us can use it successfully. In-depth information does not translate into in-depth profits. -David Dreman

211. A good rule of thumb is that once an investment reaches a double-digit yield, you're well into high-risk territory. So never start your search for new investments based on the highest yields possible... unless you just want to gamble with your money. -Dr. David Eifrig, Jr.

212. The difference between the investor who year in and year out procures for himself a final net profit, and the one who is usually in the red, is not entirely a question of superior selection of stocks or superior timing. Rather, it is also a case of knowing how to capitalize successes and curtail failures.

–Gerald Loeb

213. Someone's sitting in the shade today because someone planted a tree a long time ago.

–Warren Buffett

214. I have always believed that a single talented analyst, working very hard, can cover an amazing amount of investment landscape, and this belief remains unchallenged in my mind. -Michael Burry

215. If you spend your energies looking for and analyzing situations not closely followed by other informed investors, your chance of finding bargains greatly increases. -Joel Greenblatt

216. Only buy stocks that are cheap, hated, and in an uptrend. -Steve Sjuggerud

217. It's not the ones that you sell that keep going up that matter. It's the one that you don't sell that keep going down that does.
    –Arthur Huprich

218. One should never permit speculative ventures to run into investments.
    –Jesse Livermore

219. Often financial innovation is often just leverage in thinly veiled disguise.
    –James Montier

220. Big movements take time to develop.
    –Jesse Livermore

221. Stocks are just pieces of paper; you're not allowed to love them. You can't have emotional attachments to stocks.
—Jim Cramer

222. You only need a few good ideas to make a significant difference in a lifetime.
—Bruce Berkowitz

223. If we become increasingly humble about how little we know, we may be more eager to search.
—Sir John Templeton

224. Trade pattern recognition.
—Stuart Walton

225. Leverage cannot turn a bad investment into a good one, but it can turn a good one bad. –James Montier

226. Technical analysis is a windsock, not a crystal ball. It's a skill that improves with experience and study. Always be a student, there is always someone smarter than you! –Carl Swenlin

227. The money lost by speculation alone is small compared with the gigantic sums lost by so-called investors who have let their investments ride. –Jesse Livermore

228. Don't risk too much on one event or company.
-Stuart Walton

229. Price is what you pay. Value is what you get.
-Warren Buffett

230. Human emotion is a big enemy of the average investor and trader. Be patient and unemotional. There are periods where traders don't need to trade. -Arthur Huprich

231. Investing without research is like playing stud poker and never looking at the cards. -Peter Lynch

232. If you own a stock that's up 10% and you haven't sold any of it, you're getting piggish. If you own a stock that's up 20% and you haven't sold a sizeable portion, you're probably a pig. If you hit a double and a stock is up 100%, then you should sell half your position and play with the house's money, as long as you still believe in the stock. –Jim Cramer

233. Being a value investor means you look at the downside before looking at the upside. –Li Lu

234. If you have good stocks
and you really know them,
you'll make money if you're
patient over three years or
more. -David Dreman

235. The market does reflect
the available information,
as the professors tell us.
But just as the funhouse
mirrors don't always
accurately reflect your
weight, the markets don't
always accurately reflect
that information. Usually
they are too pessimistic
when it's bad, and too
optimistic when it's good.
-Bill Miller

236. Absent a lot of surprises, stocks are relatively predictable over twenty years. As to whether they're going to be higher or lower in two to three years, you might as well flip a coin to decide. –Peter Lynch

237. I've never bought a stock unless, in my view, it was on sale. –John Neff

238. Those who cannot adjust to change will be swept aside by it. Those who recognize change and react accordingly will benefit. –Jim Rogers

239. It is a happy circumstance that when nature gives us true burning desires, she also gives us the means to satisfy them. Those who want to win and lack skill can get someone with skill to help them. –Ed Seykota

240. Don't buy too many different securities. Better to have only a few investments which can be watched. –Bernard Baruch

241. The human side of every person is the greatest enemy of the average investor or speculator. –Jesse Livermore

242. He who lives by the crystal ball will eat shattered glass. -Ray Dalio

243. Successful investing is anticipating the anticipation of others. -John Maynard Keynes

244. Diversification, after all, is not how many different things you own, but how different the things you own are in the risks they entail. -Seth Klarman

245. Value in relation to price, not price alone, must determine your investment decisions. -Seth Klarman

246. In almost every walk of life, people buy more at lower prices; in the stock market they seem to buy more at higher prices. –James Grant

247. I make money. Nothing wrong with that. That's what I want to do. That's what I'm here to do. That's what I enjoy. –Carl Icahn

248. The elements of good trading are: (1) cutting losses, (2) cutting losses, and (3) cutting losses. If you follow these three rules, you may have a chance. –Ed Seykota

249. Warren Buffett has become one hell of a lot better investor since the day I met him, and so have I. If we had been frozen at any given stage, with the knowledge we had, the record would have been much worse than it is. So the game is to keep learning, and I don't think people are going to keep learning who don't like the learning process.
-Charlie Munger

250. If you don't keep getting better, you're going to do worse. -Jim Simons

251. Never confuse brains with a bull market.
−Humphrey Neill

252. Many an optimist has become rich by buying out a pessimist.
−Robert G. Allen

253. In investing, what is comfortable is rarely profitable. −Robert Arnott

254. If you buy a stock and it's up 7% and you can't decide whether you should take profits or not, then the tie-breaking vote should be to sell some of that stock. −Jim Cramer

255. Learn to take losses quickly, don't expect to be right all the time, and learn from your mistakes. -Arthur Huprich

256. You learn in this business... If you want a friend, get a dog. -Carl Icahn

257. When trading, remain objective. Don't have a preconceived idea or prejudice. Said another way, "the great names in trading all have the same trait: An ability to shift on a dime when the shifting time comes."
-Arthur Huprich

258. A market is the combined behavior of thousands of people responding to information, misinformation, and whim.
-Kenneth Chang

259. When most folks can't stand the thought of owning a particular kind of investment, chances are good that it's cheap... and that it's due for at least a short-term rebound.
-Brian Hunt

260. The four most dangerous words in investing are: *"this time it's different."*
-Sir John Templeton

261. The time of maximum pessimism is the best time to buy and the time of maximum optimism is the best time to sell.
    –Sir John Templeton

262. Never count on making a good sale. Have the purchase price be so attractive that even a mediocre sale gives good results. –Warren Buffett

263. Win or lose, everybody gets what they want out of the market. Some people seem to like to lose, so they win by losing money.
    –Ed Seykota

264. The most important rule of trading is to play great defense, not great offense. Every day I assume every position I have is wrong. -Paul Tudor Jones

265. There are old traders and there are bold traders, but there are very few old, bold traders. -Ed Seykota

266. Investors must never forget that Wall Street has a strong bullish bias, which coincides with its self-interest. -Seth Klarman

267. Be leery of leverage. -James Montier

268. The only ones to get hurt on a roller coaster are the jumpers. -Paul Harvey

269. The whole secret to winning and losing in the stock market is to lose the least amount possible when you're not right.
-William J. O'Neil

270. The most important single factor in shaping security markets is public psychology. -Gerald Loeb

271. Bulls make money, bears make money, and "pigs" get slaughtered.
-Arthur Huprich

272. Forget the needle, buy the haystack. –John Bogle

273. Choosing individual stocks without any idea of what you're looking for is like running through a dynamite factory with a burning match. You may live, but you're still an idiot. –Joel Greenblatt

274. Look, don't congratulate us when we buy a company, congratulate us when we sell it. Because any fool can overpay and buy a company, as long as money will last to buy it. –Henry Kravis

275. Superior investors make more money in good times than they give back in bad times. –Howard Marks

276. Finding the best person or the best organization to invest your money is one of the most important financial decisions you'll ever make. –Bill Gross

277. I become a buyer as soon as a stock makes a new high on its movement after having had a normal reaction. –Jesse Livermore

278. Anticipate, don't react. –Stuart Walton

279. I will tell you how to become rich. Close the doors. Be fearful when others are greedy. Be greedy when others are fearful. -Warren Buffett

280. Never invest in something you don't understand. -James Montier

281. Study your tax position to know when you can sell to the greatest advantage. -Bernard Baruch

282. Hear a [stock] story... analyze and buy aggressively if it feels right. -Julian Robertson

283. As many participants have come to realize from 1999 to 2010, during which the S&P 500 has made no upside progress, you can lose money even in the "best companies" if your timing is wrong. Yet, if the technical pattern dictates, you can make money on a short-term basis even in stocks that have a "mixed" fundamental opinion.
-Arthur Huprich

284. Buy when there is blood in the streets, even if the blood is your own.
-Nathan Rothschild

285. If you don't have integrity, you have nothing. You can't buy it. You can have all the money in the world, but if you are not a moral and ethical person, you really have nothing. -Henry Kravis

286. Most people, especially investors, try to get a certain percentage return, and actually secure a minus yield when properly calculated over the years. Speculators risk less and have a better chance of getting something, in my opinion. -Gerald Loeb

287. Investing should be more like watching paint dry or watching grass grow. If you want excitement, take $800 and go to Las Vegas. -Paul Samuelson

288. Those who invest only when commentators are upbeat end up paying a heavy price for meaningless reassurance. -Warren Buffett

289. I just wait until there is money lying in the corner, and all I have to do is go over there and pick it up. I do nothing in the meantime. -Jim Rogers

290. Real estate investing, even on a very small scale, remains a tried and true means of building an individual's cash flow and wealth. -Robert Kiyosak

291. There are plenty of ways to get ahead. The first is so basic I'm almost embarrassed to say it: spend less than you earn. -Paul Clitheroe

292. Don't think you can consistently buy at the bottom or sell at the top. This can rarely be consistently done. -Arthur Huprich

293. Here is part of the tradeoff with diversification: You must be diversified enough to survive bad times or bad luck so that skill and good process can have the chance to pay off over the long term. -Joel Greenblatt

294. Never invest in any idea you can't illustrate with a crayon. -Peter Lynch

295. Investors must be willing to forgo some near-term return, if necessary, as an insurance premium against unexpected and unpredictable adversity. -Seth Klarman

296. Even the best looking chart can fall apart for no apparent reason. Thus, never fall in love with a position but instead remain vigilant in managing risk and expectations. Use volume as a confirming guidepost. –Arthur Huprich

297. Trying to trade during a losing streak is emotionally devastating. Trying to play "catch-up" is lethal. –Ed Seykota

298. When reward is at its pinnacle, risk is near at hand. –John Bogle

299. Few people ever make money on tips. Beware of inside information. If there was easy money lying around, no one would be forcing it into your pocket. –Jesse Livermore

300. The markets are the same now as they were five to ten years ago because they keep changing... just like they did then. –Ed Seykota

301. Markets are strongest when they are broad and weakest when they narrow to a handful of blue-chip names. –Robert Farrell

302. *Michael [Marcus] taught me one thing that was incredibly important... He taught me that you could make a million dollars. He showed me that if you applied yourself, great things could happen. It is very easy to miss the point that you really can do it.*
–Bruce Kovner

303. *Investors that confine themselves to what they know, as difficult as that may be, have a considerable advantage over everyone else.*
–Seth Klarman

304. Most leading brokers cannot spare the time and money to research smaller stocks. You are therefore more likely to find a bargain in this relatively under-exploited area of the stock market.

–James D. Slater

305. Nothing beats a little cash in a bear market, of course, and the oldest form of cash is gold.

–James Grant

306. I am always thinking about losing money as opposed to making money.

–Paul Tudor Jones

307. Have realistic expectations.
-John Bogle

308. To suppose that the value of a common stock is determined purely by a corporation's earnings discounted by the relevant interest rates and adjusted for the marginal tax rate is to forget that people have burned witches, gone to war on a whim, risen to the defense of Joseph Stalin and believed Orson Welles when he told them over the radio that the Martians had landed.
-James Grant

309. Bear markets have three stages: sharp down, reflexive rebound and a drawn-out fundamental downtrend.

-Robert Farrell

310. It is better to be early than too late in recognizing the passing of one era, the waning of old investment favorites and the advent of a new era affording new opportunities for the investor.

-Thomas Rowe Price, Jr.

311. Be patient and wait for the fat pitch.

-James Montier

312. To the best of your ability, try to keep your priorities in line. Don't let the "greed factor" that Wall Street can generate outweigh other just as important areas of your life. Balance the physical, mental, spiritual, relational, and financial needs of life. -Arthur Huprich

313. When a stock reaches your price target, unless you get new information that causes you to move that target up, you shouldn't think the stock is going much higher. -Jim Cramer

314. Know what you own, and know why you own it.
   –Peter Lynch

315. As I said, there is nothing wrong with failing. Pick yourself up and try it again. You never are going to know how good you really are until you go out and face failure.
   –Henry Kravis

316. Most people ignore probabilities and exaggerate risk. –Ralph Wagner

317. If you are unsure about a position, just get out.
   –Stuart Walton

318. Historically, there has been a bull market in commodities every 20 or 30 years. –Jim Rogers

319. There is a saying, *"A picture is worth a thousand words."* One might paraphrase this by saying a profit is worth more than endless alibis or explanations... prices and trends are really the best and simplest "indicators" you can find. –Gerald Loeb

320. Risk isn't a number and it isn't volatility, it's the permanent impairment of capital. –James Montier

321. Be totally flexible; be able to admit when you are wrong. –Stuart Walton

322. I'm only rich because I know when I'm wrong... I basically have survived by recognizing my mistakes. –George Soros

323. You adapt, evolve, compete or die. –Paul Tudor Jones

324. Confronted with a challenge to distill the secret of sound investment into three words, we venture the motto, MARGIN OF SAFETY. –Benjamin Graham

325. Be realistic about the downside of an investment; expect the worst case to be much more severe than you anticipated.
–David Dreman

326. Almost all of our best-performing investments are low-risk. That means these were investments in big, dominant, slower-growing businesses with good balance sheets and brands. –Porter Stansberry

327. It is simple to see what is necessary, but not easy to be willing or able to do it.
–Howard Marks

328. I rely a great deal on animal instincts. –George Soros

329. I don't know too many people that are good at timing the market relative to macro-economic events. –Joel Greenblatt

330. It's one of the most important things at the end of the day; being able to say no to an investment. –Henry Kravis

331. Every debt is ultimately paid, if not by the debtor, then eventually by the creditor. –James Grant

332. Wishful thinking must be banished. –Jesse Livermore

333. Playing by the rules, one does the best he can, irrespective of the social consequences. Whereas in making the rules, people ought to be concerned with the social consequences and not with their personal interests. –George Soros

334. The older I get, the more I see a straight path in where I want to go. If you're going to hunt elephants, don't get off the trail for a rabbit.
–T. Boone Pickens

335. Value investing requires a great deal of hard work, unusually strict discipline, and a long-term investment horizon.
–Seth Klarman

336. My experience indicates that most people who've accumulated a great deal of wealth haven't had that as their goal at all. Wealth is only a by-product, not the original motivation.
–Michael Milken

337. You don't need analysts in a bull market, and you don't want them in a bear market. –Gerald Loeb

338. Wishful thinking can be detrimental to your financial wealth.
-Arthur Huprich

339. It is generally agreed that casinos should, in the public interest, be inaccessible and expensive. And perhaps the same is true of stock exchanges.
-John Maynard Keynes

340. The best investment opportunities arise when other investors act unwisely, thereby creating rewards for those who act intelligently.
-Seth Klarman

341. Have the courage of your convictions. –John Griffin

342. Any dead fish can go with the flow. Yet, it takes a strong fish to swim against the flow. In other words, what seems "hard" at the time is usually, over time, right. –Arthur Huprich

343. Financial peace isn't the acquisition of stuff. It's learning to live on less than you make, so you can give money back and have money to invest. You can't win until you do this.
–Dave Ramsey

344. What we try to do is take advantage of errors others make, usually because they are too short-term oriented, or they react to dramatic events, or they overestimate the impact of events, and so on.
–Bill Miller

345. If there's one thing income investors should constantly remember, it's buy value. By that, I mean you should always pay a fair price for what something is worth.
–Dr. David Eifrig, Jr.

346. There's no escaping risk.
–John Bogle

347. Exponentially rapidly rising or falling markets usually go further than you think, but they do not correct by going sideways.
   -Robert Farrell

348. If you are going to be a great investor, you have to fit the style to who you are. -Michael Burry

349. It is a warning flag if the market is not responding to data correctly.
   -Stuart Walton

350. Time is your friend; impulse is your enemy.
   -John Bogle

351. It's always better for you to cut your losses and sell damaged goods in order to buy a stock you have more conviction in. –Jim Cramer

352. You will be wrong often; recognize winners and losers fast. –Stuart Walton

353. There are no new eras... excesses are never permanent. –Robert Farrell

354. If you are shopping for common stocks, choose them the way you would buy groceries, not the way you would buy perfume. –Benjamin Graham

355. Value investors — who buy at a discount from underlying value — are in a position to take advantage of Mr. Market's irrationality.
-Seth Klarman

356. Progress is cumulative in science and engineering, but cyclical in finance.
-James Grant

357. A climate of fear is an investor's best friend... big opportunities come infrequently. When it's raining gold, reach for a bucket, not a thimble.
-Warren Buffett

358. I feel all relevant factors, important and otherwise, are registered in the market's behavior, and in addition, the action of the market itself can be expected under most circumstances to stimulate buying or selling in a manner consistent enough to allow reasonably accurate forecasting of news in advance of its actual occurrence.
–Gerald Loeb

359. Intellectual capital will always trump financial capital. –Paul Tudor Jones

360. The price of a commodity will never go to zero. When you invest in commodities futures, you're not buying a piece of paper that says you own an intangible piece of a company that can go bankrupt.
–Jim Rogers

361. There are two hedges I know of: one is cash and the other is knowledge.
–Bruce Berkowitz

362. Fear is a stronger emotion than hope, which is why bear markets are always swifter than bull markets.
–Elliott Wave International

363. Commandment #1: Thou Shall Not Trade Against the Trend. -P. Arthur Huprich

364. My view is that an investor is better off knowing a lot about a few investments than knowing a little about each of a great many holdings. One's very best ideas are likely to generate higher returns for a given level of risk than one's hundredth or thousandth best idea. -Seth Klarman

365. Never buy a stock because it has had a big decline from its previous high. -Jesse Livermore

366. A majority of life's errors are caused by forgetting what one is really trying to do. -Charlie Munger

367. Change is the investor's only certainty.
-Thomas Rowe Price, Jr.

368. Our mandate is to find the 200 best companies in the world and invest in them, and find the 200 worst companies in the world and go short on them. If the 200 best don't do better than the 200 worst, you should probably be in another business.
-Julian Robertson

369. *Risk* is the permanent loss of capital, never a number. –James Montier

370. All market fads come to an end. Security prices eventually become too high, supply catches up with and then exceeds demand, the top is reached, and the downward slide ensues. There will always be cycles of investment fashion and just as surely investors who are susceptible to them. –Seth Klarman

371. A pile of junk is still junk no matter how you stack it. –Seth Klarman

372. If a man didn't make mistakes, he'd own the world in a month. But if he didn't profit by his mistakes, he wouldn't own a blessed thing.
  -Jesse Livermore

373. In baseball, you can hit 40 home runs on a single A-league team and never get paid a thing. But in a hedge fund, you get paid on your batting average. So you go to the worst league you can find, where there's the least competition.
  -Julian Robertson

374. Money cannot consistently be made trading every day or every week during the year. –Jesse Livermore

375. Risk no more than you can afford to lose, and also risk enough so that a win is meaningful. –Ed Seykota

376. Prices move before fundamentals. –Stuart Walton

377. Invest in high-return businesses run for the shareholders. –Lou Simpson

378. You have to get rid of the fear of selling a position. –Jeff Clark

379. Whatever task you undertake, do it with all your heart and soul. Always be courteous, never be discouraged. Beware of him who promises something for nothing. Do not blame anybody for your mistakes and failures. Do not look for approval except the consciousness of doing your best.
–Bernard Baruch

380. The stock market is filled with individuals who know the price of everything, but the value of nothing.
–Philip Fisher

381. Accounting was the course that helped me more than anything.

-Julian Robertson

382. The borrowers will always be willing to take a great deal for themselves. It's up to the lenders to show restraint, and when they lose it, watch out.

-Michael Burry

383. Like Warren, I had a considerable passion to get rich, not because I wanted Ferrari's... I wanted the independence. I desperately wanted it.

-Charlie Munger

384. If we do well for the client, we'll be taken care of.

−Thomas Rowe Price, Jr.

385. Always keep a good part of your capital in a cash reserve. Never invest all your funds.

−Bernard Baruch

386. Most of the time stocks are subject to irrational and excessive price fluctuations in both directions as the consequence of the ingrained tendency of most people to speculate or gamble... to give way to hope, fear and greed.

−Benjamin Graham

387. The public buys the most at the top and the least at the bottom. –Robert Farrell

388. The leaders of today may not be the leaders of two years from now.
–Jesse Livermore

389. Wall Street's graveyards are filled with men who were right too soon.
–William Hamilton

390. If you want to have a better performance than the crowd, you must do things differently from the crowd.
–Sir John Templeton

391. The financial markets offer many temptations to vulnerable investors. It is easy to do the wrong thing, to speculate rather than invest. Emotion lies dangerously close to the surface for most investors and can be particularly intense when market prices move drastically in either direction. It is crucial that investors understand and learn to take advantage of the opportunities presented by Mr. Market.

-Seth Klarman

392. Don't buy a stock simply because it has had a big decline from its high and is now a "better value"; wait for the market to recognize "value" first. -Arthur Huprich

393. Don't speculate unless you can make it a full-time job. -Bernard Baruch

394. Investors must learn to resist fear, the tendency to panic when prices are falling, greed, and the tendency to become overly enthusiastic when prices are rising. -Seth Klarman

395. Rule One: Never lose money. Rule Two: Never forget rule number one. -Warren Buffett

396. Hope sustains life, but misplaced hope prolongs recessions. -James Grant

397. The market can stay irrational longer than you can stay solvent. -John Maynard Keynes

398. The most important quality for an investor is temperament, not intellect. -Warren Buffett

399. It's not whether you're right or wrong that's important, but how much money you make when you're right and how much you lose when you're wrong. -George Soros

Well, you have reached the end of this book. It has been very difficult trying to narrow it down to my favorite quotes of all time. I hope that these quotes helped you on days where you needed an extra boost to maximize your success.

P.S. I added in a couple of bonus quotes for you, mostly because I couldn't get all the way down to the final 365. I hope you enjoyed them! :)

This book is also available for digital download if you would like to keep it on your phone or tablet for quick reference or for a little pocket motivation.

Please visit us at www.littlebookofquotes.com

9 781535 015165